When The Silence Screamed

Healed, But Not Unscarred

Sherri Carter

Copyright

When the Silence Screamed: Healed but Not Unscarred © 2025 Sherri Carter

All rights reserved.

ISBN: 979-8-218-83120-2

No part of this publication may be reproduced, distributed, or transmitted in any form by any means, electronic, mechanical, photocopying, recording, or otherwise, without the written permission of the author, exception of the author, except in the case of brief quotations used in critical reviews or scholarly works.

This is a work of nonfiction based on the author's personal experiences. Some of the names and identifying details have been changed to protect the privacy of individuals.

Edited By: Tina Adams-Turnipseed

DEDICATION

For those who are still silently suffering.
For the ones carrying invisible wounds, silent screams, and memories that still shake your soul.
This book is for you.

For the women who have survived abandonment, betrayal, grief, and trauma, you are not alone.
For those that have ever felt invisible, unworthy, or silenced, may these pages give voice to your healing.
This book is for you.

And to the one I lost, I loved you then, I love you still, and I carry your memory as I choose to live.

Table Of Contents

Acknowledgements

Introduction: Why I'm Telling My Story

Section 1: The Silence

1. Abandoned But Still Breathing
2. Living Numb
3. The Love I Never Saw

   ■ What I needed from my Parents

   ■ Letter to My Mother

   ■ Letter to My Father

   ■ Letter to my Paternal Grandmother

Section 2: The Breaking

4. The Moment I Broke

5. The Moment that Finally Broke Me
6. Shadows of His Mind
7. The Day Everything Changed

8. Night After the Trauma
9. When The Silence Got Too Loud
10. Therapy, Tears, and Truth

    ■ Letter to My Son

11. A Mother's Love Beyond Loss

    ■ Letter to my Mother in Love

12. Love in the Shadows

- ■ How can you teach love and still withhold it
- 💔 To the man who couldn't show up
- 🌟 From the season of vulnerability
- ■ To the Me that stayed strong

Section 3: The Healing

13. Unlearning Survival
14. The Return to Myself
15. Healing Isn't Pretty, But it's Sacred
16. Rewriting the Story
17. The Girl Who Came Back to Life
18. Becoming the Woman I Needed

- ■ Letter to my Maternal Grandmother
- ■ Letter to my Paternal Grandfather

In Loving Memory

Journal With Me: Pain on Paper

Reflection Note Pages

ACKNOWLEDGMENTS

To God, thank you for carrying me through the darkest valleys and for never letting go of my hand, even when I wanted to let go of life. This book is a reflection of your grace and healing power.

To my maternal grandmother, your love raised me, your strength sustained me, and your spirit still surrounds me. You taught me how to keep going even when I didn't want to. This book carries legacy.

To my son, you are the reason I chose to heal instead of hurt others. Watching you grow gave me the courage to break the cycles that once tried to break me. I pray this book helps you understand the strength of your mother.

To family, friends and strangers who held space for my truth, you may never know what your words, presence, or prayers did for me. But I felt them and I'm grateful.

To my former self, I thank you for surviving long enough to become the woman you were always meant to be. I see you. I honor you. I love you.

And to anyone holding pain in silence, I wrote this book so you wouldn't have to suffer anymore.

Introduction
"Why I'm Telling My Story"

I am telling my story because silence almost destroyed me. For too long, I carried pain I thought no one would understand, trauma that I tried to bury, abandonment I tried to ignore, grief that I tried to outrun. There were days I didn't think I'd survive. Days when the pain was louder than my prayers, and the silence of abandonment echoed louder than any voice of love. I've walked through heartbreak, betrayal, loss, and moments of deep emotional trauma that nearly shattered me. Silence only made the weight heavier. I thank God that I'm still here.

This book is my way of breaking that silence. It is my pain on paper, but also my healing. I am telling my story because there are still too many people still suffering silently, still carrying invisible wounds, still believing they are alone.

I want my words to be a hand reaching into the darkness for someone else, to remind you that your story matters, that your scars are not shameful, and that healing is possible even when it feels far away.

This book is not about perfection, it's about truth. It's about a woman who was broken, overlooked, and left behind, but who chose to rise. This is my story. I'm telling it to the ones who are still crying silently, still pretending they're okay, still looking for a way to breathe again.

You are not alone, and this is proof that healing is possible.

Section 1: The Silence

CHAPTER 1
"ABANDONED BUT STILL BREATHING"

Abandonment doesn't always look like someone walking out the door. Sometimes, it looks like people staying, but not showing up for you. I've experienced both. There were people who promised they'd be there forever. Family, friends, and partners, who disappeared when I needed them most. There were others who stayed physically, but emotionally? They were long gone.

One of the hardest lessons I had to learn was that just because someone should love you, doesn't mean they will, and just because you love them deeply, doesn't mean they'll know how to love you back.

I started carrying that rejection like it was my identity. I thought maybe I wasn't lovable, maybe I was too broken, too emotional, too much. It took years for me to realize that I wasn't the problem.

They didn't know how to hold me because they'd never learned how to hold themselves. They didn't know how to see me because they never learned to look inward. That realization didn't erase the hurt, but it gave me space to breathe again.

I started asking myself, "What would it look like to stop chasing people who only loved me in pieces?" And the answer was clear, that I needed to start loving myself as a whole.

CHAPTER 2
"LIVING NUMB"

There's a silence that hurts worse than screaming. I remember walking through my days like a ghost. Smiling when I needed to. Nodding when people spoke. Laughing on cue. But inside? I was gone. That's what emotional numbness feels like. It's not always tears or tantrums, it's the quiet absence of everything, even pain. I didn't want to feel anything anymore, because every time I opened my heart, it got broken again. I shut down. I stopped trusting. I stopped hoping. I started surviving. I became the strong one. The "I'm fine" one. The "I don't need anybody" one. But deep down, I was just scared to be vulnerable.

I wanted someone to see through the mask, to say, "I know you're not okay, and I'm not going anywhere." But no one ever did. So, I got used to hiding behind busyness, distractions, and numbness.

I wasn't healing, I was just avoiding it. Eventually, all that pretending became too heavy to carry. That's when I began to ask myself: What would it cost me to feel again? To be honest? To let the broken parts breathe?

That question…**was the beginning of everything.**

CHAPTER 3
"THE LOVE I NEVER SAW"

I was only a teenager when life handed me a responsibility far too heavy for my young shoulders, to care for my paternal grandmother. She wasn't the soft spoken, gentle presence that most people associate with grandmothers. She was an alcoholic. She was belligerent and unpredictable. She was a woman who lived more in the bottom of the bottle than in the real world around her.

My grandfather drove trucks for a living, and most of the time he was on the road. His long hauls kept him away for weeks at a time, leaving me with her as my constant reality. There was no shield, no buffer, no one to step in when her drinking spiraled out of control. His absence wasn't intentional neglect, he was working to provide, but it meant that I was left alone to face the storm.

Her drink of choice was Canadian LTD, hidden under the bathroom sink inside the cabinet. I can still picture the way she would disappear into that bathroom completely sober, close the door, and then emerge minutes later, slurring, staggering, and transformed into someone unrecognizable. That bottle was her secret companion, but it was no secret to me. It was the switch that turned the grandmother I wanted into the torment I dreaded. Her words, sharp and cutting when she was drunk, left scars that lingered long after the echoes of her voice faded. Sometimes I wondered if she saw me at all, or if I was just another body in the room to lash out at when the alcohol took over. And yet, despite her recklessness, I couldn't walk away. Blood tied me to her, and loyalty chained me to the duty of caring for her.

In those years I learned resilience the hard way. I learned to shield myself emotionally. I learned how heavy it feels when the roles of caregiver and child are reversed.

Looking back, I see that my paternal grandmother's addiction was her escape from her own pain, even if it destroyed everything around her. My grandfather's long hours on the road, though out of duty and survival, meant that I bore the brunt of the destruction alone. I was her keeper.

Those memories are jagged, but they also shaped me. They taught me that sometimes love feels like survival, and family ties can both bind and break you. My paternal grandmother's chaos was not the foundation I needed, but it was the storm that forced me to grow strong roots, even in broken soil.

I had a father, but he wasn't a daddy. He was also an alcoholic. Loud when he drank, mean when he spoke, and even though he was physically there at times, emotionally he was nowhere to be found. He never knew my son. Not sure if he really cared too. And that alone, left a scar that I still carry today. Watching him reject and ignore his grandchild reopened wounds I didn't even know were still bleeding. How could he look into the eyes of innocence and offer nothing but coldness? I didn't just grieve the love I didn't get as I got older, I grieved the love I wanted him to give to my son. He said cruel things when he was drunk, words that cut deeper than fists. He didn't know how to love. He didn't know how to affirm. He taught me that not all wounds are visible, and not all pain is easy to explain.

I used to wonder why my father couldn't love me the way I needed. Why his words were sharp, his presence heavy, his affection distant.

As I grew older, I realized his story didn't begin with him, it began with what he inherited. My father watched his own mother drown in addiction. He witnessed the damage alcohol could do to a home, to a heart, to a family, and yet somehow, he carried that same burden into his own life.

His addiction wasn't just his, it was a chain passed down, generation to generation. He didn't ask for it, but he didn't know how to break it either.

I believed that he did love me but had a difficult way of showing it at times. He tried in his own broken way, but the bottle was louder than my cries. The alcohol was stronger than his intentions. And the man he could have been was drowned out by the man the addiction made him be.

I longed for a father who would see me, hold me, protect me. Instead, I was left with a man who numbed himself instead of facing his pain. His words, soaked in liquor, cut deeper than any absence could. In the end, his struggle with addiction claimed his life.

He taught me something without meaning to, how cycles destroy relationships, and how desperately they need to be broken. But the cycle stops with me.

My mother? She was there when I was a child but in my teenage years when I needed my mother the most, she walked away without me. One day she was there, and the next she was gone. She moved in with her boyfriend and I stayed behind with her mom. No warning. No closure. Just absence.

I kept asking myself; What did I do wrong? Why wasn't I worth staying for?

That kind of abandonment doesn't just hurt, it shapes you. It teaches you not to trust. Not to depend on anyone. Not to expect too much from anyone, but God didn't leave me alone.

Both of my parents taught me a painful kind of lesson; that people who are supposed to love you, may not know how and mourning relationships that never became what you needed them to be and that's grief of its own. I want to thank God for my maternal grandmother. My maternal grandmother stepped in. She picked up the pieces they left behind. She mothered me when my mother didn't. She shielded me when my father wouldn't. She loved me, not perfectly but presently. She wasn't supposed to be raising another child but she did.

With love.
With consistency.
With sacrifice.

    I carry her legacy in the way I show up for my son. I am a safe place for him that I didn't have. I am the soft landing they never gave me. I am the love I never saw, and that is healing. I lost both my parents in different ways growing up. I lost my father to addiction and emotional distance. Though my mother is alive today, in that chapter of my life I lost her presence to abandonment. What felt like loss in those years gave me clarity for the woman I would become. I became a mother who breaks the cycle. I became the voice that speaks where silence once lived. I became the kind of love I never saw.

And that to me is redemption.

Journal Entry
"WHAT I NEEDED FROM MY PARENTS"

I needed safety. I needed a soft place to land. Arms that didn't push me away. Words that didn't bruise. Eyes that looked at me like I mattered. From my mother, I needed presence. I needed her to stay. I needed her to choose me over a man. To show me that I was worth more than being left behind. To protect me, fight for me, see me, but she left and that silence screamed louder than any goodbye.

From my father, I needed gentleness. I needed someone to call me beautiful, smart, worthy. I needed a man to show me what love looked like so I wouldn't go searching for it in all the wrong places. Instead, I got slurred words and sharp insults. I got a drunk version of a man who never became who I needed him to be.

I needed both of them to say "I'm proud of you". To apologize for not showing up to my high school graduation. To apologize for not trying to help me succeed in life. I needed them to hold me when I cried instead of being the reason for my tears.

I needed consistency. Love that didn't leave when things got hard. Love that wasn't loud and hurtful or quiet and missing. But I never got those things when I needed them the most. So, I learned how to give them to myself. I became the love I longed for. I became the presence I never had. I became a soft place for my son, so he would never have to write these same words about me.

Now my mother is here, and even though I'll never get those lost years back, I see her trying. She's trying to show up, trying to make space in my life again, trying to hold me in ways she couldn't before, and that means something.

That's healing too.

Letter to My Mother

Dear Mama,

I want you to know how much I love you.

There were years when I didn't understand why you left. I carried that pain quietly, believing it meant something was wrong with me. But over time, I've learned that your leaving wasn't about me, it was about your own battles, your own journey, your own choices. And even though it hurts, I forgive you. Forgiveness doesn't erase the past, but it frees me from carrying the weight of it and I don't take it for granted.

Thank you for being here. Thank you for trying. Thank you for loving me, even if it looks different from what I once imagined.

Mama, I want you to know this: you matter to me. Your presence now matters. And I appreciate you.

Thank you for being here. Thank you for trying. Thank you for loving me in the ways you can today.

I love you, deeply, always.
And I forgive you.

Love,
Your Daughter

Letter to My Father

Dear Daddy,

You were not the father I needed you to be when you drank. Your words wounded me. Your silence scarred me. Your addiction stole moments that can never be returned. But today, I choose to let go.

Not because you asked for forgiveness.
Not because the pain disappeared.
But because I am tired of carrying it.

I know now that you were hurting too. That the love you couldn't give me was the same love you never received yourself. I wish things had been different. I wish you had shown up more. I wish you had seen me and my son through the eyes of love. But today, I released the weight. I forgive you, not because you earned it, but because I deserve it.

I am healing. I am choosing peace, and I am no longer waiting on love from the grave. I forgive you. I release you. I live for myself now.

Your Daughter
Sherri

Letter to My Paternal Grandmother

Dear Grandma,

There are words I've held inside for so long, unsure if I could ever truly say them. But today, I want to speak to you from a place of honesty and love.

Growing up, I often longed for your presence in a way I couldn't always explain. There were times when alcohol stood between us, and it left me feeling like I lost pieces of you even while you were still here. As a child, I didn't understand why, but I knew I wanted more of your love, your attention, your consistency.

Those memories left me with hurt, and for a long time, I carried that weight. But today, I choose something different, I choose forgiveness.

I forgive you, Grandma. I forgive you for the moments when your pain spoke louder than your love. I forgive you for not being able to give me all that I needed. And I forgive you because I know now that you were fighting battles bigger than me, battles that began long before I was even born.

You are still here, and so am I. That means we still have time, time to love, time to share, time to heal. I don't want to carry resentment; I want to carry peace. I want you to know that despite everything, I love you.

This is not just forgiveness for you, Grandma, it's freedom for me. And it's my way of breaking the cycle so that I can live, love, and heal differently.

With compassion and love,

Your Granddaughter

Section 2: The Breaking

CHAPTER 4
"THE MOMENT I BROKE"

There wasn't one single moment when everything fell apart. There were hundreds. One day it all came crashing down. I was standing in the kitchen doing something as ordinary as washing the dishes. The sound of running water, the clinking of a plate, the hum of life trying to carry on, everything felt normal. But it wasn't.

I was exhausted. Tired in a way even sleep couldn't fix and hollow in a way I didn't have words for. Then, just like that, I broke. I dropped the plate, and it shattered. The sound startled me, but it wasn't the glass that made me fall to the floor, it was everything I had been holding in.

Every scream, I swallowed.
Every tear, I never let fall.
Every "I'm fine" I forced out through trembling lips.

I collapsed in that kitchen like my body finally got permission to feel what my heart had been carrying for years. I wept loud, guttural sobs, the kind that sound like survival cracking open. I didn't care who heard me, I wasn't trying to be strong anymore. I wasn't trying to hold it together for anyone. In that moment, I met the version of myself I had buried beneath survival.

I was broken and I was tired of pretending I wasn't.

It happened slowly, painfully, and almost quietly. I was smiling on the outside, but inside, I was crumbling. The kind of pain I carried couldn't be seen, it lived in my chest, in my thoughts, in the way I started to feel numb around people who once brought me joy. I trusted people who walked away. I loved people who didn't love me back. I showed up for everyone…but no one showed up for me.

The truth is, it wasn't just his mental illness that broke him. It broke me, too. I watched the man I loved slip away, piece by piece, thought by thought. His paranoia became my prison. His fear became my silence. His confusion became my exhaustion.

Every day, I tried to be strong for him, for us, for our son, but love doesn't protect you from being wounded by someone else's suffering. His pain seeped into me until I was carrying both of our burdens, and in trying to hold him together, I was slowly falling apart.

That was the moment I realized: silence doesn't mean strength. Sometimes silence is a cage, and I was done living in it. That breakdown? It became the start of my breakthrough. I didn't know how I was going to heal. I didn't have a plan, but I knew one thing. I didn't want to live like that anymore. I didn't know how I was going to heal. I didn't have a plan.

I remember sitting in my room, staring at the walls, asking God, "What did I do to deserve this?"

CHAPTER 5
"THE MOMENT THAT FINALLY BROKE ME"

It didn't happen all at once. Mental illness doesn't always knock loudly; it tiptoes in quietly and starts stealing pieces of the person you love.

One day the man I loved for 20 years and the father of my son was himself and suddenly something was different. He paced more, he got more paranoid, he slept less, and he stared off into places I couldn't follow.

At first, I thought maybe he was just tired or stressed, and trying to carry too much but didn't know how to say it. The silence started stretching longer and the paranoia got worse. The weight in the room got heavier every time he walked into it. That's when the fear settled in. It was like I was living with a stranger.

I watched the man I loved start slipping away from me, one unspoken word at a time. No matter how tightly I tried to hold on, I couldn't stop what was happening. I couldn't fix it even though I tried. I couldn't reach him, and that broke me.

Loving someone with a broken mind feels like screaming underwater. It's loud in your chest but no one else could hear it. You start questioning everything. "Did I miss the signs?" "Could I have stopped this?" "What did I do wrong?" The truth is, I didn't cause it so I couldn't control it, but I felt every ounce of it.

That was the moment I broke. The moment I realized the person I loved wasn't coming back the way I knew him. The mental illness wasn't just affecting him, it was swallowing me, too. And still I stayed because I loved him. I held on and I tried to help him through his struggles.

CHAPTER 6
"SHADOWS OF HIS MIND"

The day I took him to the hospital broke me in a way I didn't know was possible. He wasn't himself anymore. His eyes darted around the room, filled with fear. His words were scattered, paranoid, broken pieces of thoughts made no sense. I wanted to hold him, to calm him, but love couldn't quiet what was happening inside his mind.

He was put on a 72-hour psychiatric hold. I stood there as the doors closed behind him, my hands shaking, my heart screaming silently. It felt like betrayal, even though I knew it was for his safety. He was mine, and yet at that moment, I couldn't reach him.

For three days, I lived in prayer. I begged God to bring him back to me, the man who laughed, who dreamed, and who made me feel safe. I felt as though God had failed me. When he was released from the hospital, he wasn't the same. His eyes were distant, his spirit confused. He looked at me, but it was like he couldn't see me.

That night, I cried silently beside him. I prayed I wouldn't have to take him back, prayed that life could somehow return to normal. But deep down, I knew normal was gone.

Every day after that, life became difficult. He walked through life carrying a weight I couldn't see but I could feel pressing down on both of us. Paranoia shadowed him, and I watched him suffer, powerless to pull him out.

He tried to show up. He tried to be present for me, for our family, for life. The joy he once carried so naturally was gone. He could no longer enjoy life the way he had before the illness took hold. His laughter didn't sound the same, and the spark in his eyes was dimmed by fear and confusion. It was like watching someone you love drown in slow motion, while you stand on the shore screaming their name.

And that was the beginning of the end.

CHAPTER 7
"THE DAY EVERYTHING CHANGED"

It was supposed to be an ordinary day, but nothing about it was ordinary. I never imagined the man I loved would die right in front of me. And not just die but choose to leave this world in a way that shattered my mind, my heart, and my soul all at once. That morning, he was restless. He paced the floor nervously, and I knew something wasn't right. I could feel it in my bones. The kind of tension that settles in the air and won't leave.

He went into the garage several times, once to smoke a cigarette, another time to take out the trash, but I could see the weight in his eyes. Something was heavy in him, something deeper than I could fix. I picked up the phone and called his mother. I told her that I was worried and that something wasn't normal. Moments later, she pulled into the driveway. As I opened the garage door, he stood there on the other side of the garage about two car lengths from me, staring directly into my eyes with the gun in his hand, weeping and apologizing for what he was about to do. I was at the garage control and as I hit the button to open it, praying that letting in the light and him seeing his mother would change the outcome. But it didn't. It happened so fast. One moment, we were in the middle of a storm, emotionally, maybe verbally, but I still loved him. I still thought we'd make it through. That single moment broke something inside me that I didn't know could break.

When I saw the gun, I screamed "PLEASE DON'T DO THIS!" It was a flashing light and a loud bang as he put the gun to his head and pulled the trigger. Then there was silence, but it wasn't silent for too long. That single moment broke something inside me that I didn't know could break. I heard screams, not just mine, but his mothers, and our son. This was a scream that I had never heard before and I still can't forget it. As I ran downstairs to our son trying to keep him from coming upstairs to the chaos as I was dialing 911 with shaking hands. His cries echoed through the house like a warning, like a wound, like the truth that this wasn't a nightmare. I was awake, and this was real. I was trying to speak clearly to the dispatcher, but I could barely breathe. I kept thinking about the man that I loved was gone while listening to our child scream, terrified, confused, and broken open as I held him tight. I wanted to make sure that our child didn't see his father in that state. It wasn't one life that ended in that garage. A piece of all of us died that day. But how do you protect a child from trauma when you're drowning in it yourself? I felt helpless. Like a failure. I loved a man who couldn't love himself enough to stay, and our son heard it happen.

For a long time, I blamed myself. I carried the guilt of not saving him. The guilt of what our son heard. The guilt of how loud that gunshot was, and how it still echoes in both of us. I've had to learn that his decision wasn't my fault. That his pain was deeper than my love could reach. I still love him. I always will. I had to choose to live for me and for our child. Healing from that trauma hasn't been linear. Some days, I still hear the sound. I still hear our child's scream. Now, I will speak about it. I will write about it. I refuse to carry it in silence anymore. He is gone but I thank God that we are still breathing. I owe it to both of us to keep healing forward.

I tried to save him. I tried to hold it together. But in that moment, everything changed.

CHAPTER 8
"Night after the Trauma"

The house was filled with silence, but it wasn't peaceful, it was haunting. Every shadow in the corner felt too loud, too sharp, too close. I couldn't close my eyes. Every time I blinked, I saw it again, his eyes staring at me, the sound of the bang, the way everything shifted in a single second. I replayed it repeatedly, begging my mind to stop. "My ears are still ringing. My body is frozen. I keep seeing it, over and over again. The blood, the sound, and the look in his eyes before it happened. I don't know how I'm still breathing but I don't know if I want to be. I want to scream but no sound comes out. I want someone to hold me and say it's going to be okay, but I know it won't be. Not now because he's gone and I watched him go. My house didn't feel safe anymore. My skin didn't feel safe anymore. My own thoughts didn't feel safe anymore.

I wanted to scream.
I wanted to run.
But I couldn't leave at that moment.

I had to live in that space for a few more months before I could escape the atmosphere. The night after the trauma wasn't about surviving the memory. It was about realizing that surviving it had become my only choice. I knew this truth: nothing would ever erase what happened, but for the sake of my son and myself, I had to keep breathing. The night broke me wide open and marked the beginning of my fight to live again. So, I sat there numb and shaking, staring at the wall until the sun came up.

That was the first night I truly understood what it meant to be broken.

CHAPTER 9
"WHEN THE SILENCE GOT TOO LOUD"

After he died, I couldn't hear silence the same way. It used to be peaceful, but now it screams. The silence reminded me of that moment, the moment after the gunshot, when the world froze and I realized nothing would ever be the same again. For a while, I stopped speaking. I went quiet, not just with my mouth, but with my spirit. I was angry. I didn't trust people. I didn't trust my own judgement. I didn't feel safe in rooms where there were loud noises or sudden movements. I couldn't talk about it, not really, because every time I tried, it felt like I was reliving it. But silence wasn't helping me anymore, it was trapping me.

One night I remember lying in bed and thinking, "If I keep everything bottled up, it's going to kill me, too." That's when I started writing. Not for anyone else but for me. I wrote letters I never planned to send. I cried onto journal pages. I started saying out loud what I had been keeping inside.

"I'm angry."
"I'm scared."
"I miss him."
"I wish I could forget."

I couldn't pray at first, I didn't know how. I didn't trust God anymore. But eventually, my cries became prayers. Healing didn't come all at once. It came in pieces. A deep breath. A therapy session. A sunrise that reminded me that I was still here. I began talking to people again. Safe people. People who didn't try to fix me, but who sat with me in the dark. I learned that healing doesn't mean forgetting. It means remembering without reliving. I still have hard days, loud days, days when the silence creeps back in. I don't run from it anymore, I face it, I speak through it. And every time I tell the truth about what happened, the silence loses a little more power over me.

CHAPTER 10
"THERAPY, TEARS, AND TRUTH"

I didn't want to go to therapy at first. I thought it meant I was weak, broken and out of control. But the truth was, I was broken. I was out of control. I was mad and the world. I just didn't want to admit it. The grief, the trauma, the guilt was eating at me from the inside out. Trying to heal by myself was like putting a Band-Aid on a bullet wound. I finally walked into that room, arms crossed, heart guarded, eyes full of tears I didn't want to cry. Walking into therapy felt like walking into a battlefield with no armor. I was scared to let anyone see the cracks I had hidden for so long. Therapy demanded honesty, the kind I had never given myself before. For the first time I heard someone say, "It's okay to fall apart. That's how we begin again."

I cried like I hadn't cried in years. I spoke about the things I'd kept buried. I admitted the nightmares, the panic attacks, the guilt, the anger, the moments I didn't want to live. Piece by piece, session by session, I started finding words for the pain I thought had no language. It wasn't easy, some days, I left therapy more tired than I went in. Healing is work, it's truth telling, it's grieving without shame.

I started reconnecting with my body. I learned how trauma lives in the nervous system. How to breathe deeply. How to recognize triggers, and how to soothe myself without going numb.

I learned that healing didn't mean forgetting him. It meant forgiving myself. It meant honoring my grief and my growth. I still have bad days, but I no longer carry them alone.

Therapy gave me my voice back. Tears gave me permission to feel again. And the truth? Truth saved my life.

Letter to My Son

My Precious Son,

Before you ever took your first breath, you already had a place in my heart that no one else could touch, and from that moment I held you, I knew you were my reason to keep going. There were days when I didn't think I would make it, moments when the pain was so heavy that I didn't see a way out. I would hear your voice, or see your face, and I'd remember that I had something worth living for and someone worth fighting for.

You saved me without even knowing it. You gave my life meaning during seasons where I had none. You brought light into places that were once full of darkness. You gave me the courage to heal when I wanted to stay broken.

You are the best gift your father ever gave me. Even though his story ended too soon, and the pain of that day will always live in my memory, you are the beauty that came from the brokenness. You are the part of him I still get to hold, love, and raise with purpose.

I know I haven't been perfect. There are things I'm still working on. One thing I can say without question is that I have loved you with everything I had.

Even when I was tired.
Even when I was hurting.
Even when I didn't know how to love myself, I loved you.

You have taught me so much about patience, resilience, softness and what it means to keep showing up for someone, even when life has tried to break you.

You are not just my son.

You are my miracle.
My legacy.
My greatest victory.

If there's one thing I want you to always remember, it's this;

You are loved. You are wanted. You are enough.

I will always be here rooting for you, fighting for you, and loving you, no matter what.

With all my heart,
Mom
Healed but not unscarred

CHAPTER 11
"A Mother's Love Beyond Loss"

When I lost the love of my life, she lost her son. Two different heartbreaks, but both rooted in the same man we loved.

I often wonder how she carried that weight, burying her child. A pain no mother should ever know, no heart should ever bear. And yet, in the middle of her grief, she didn't close off. She opened wider.

She loved me. She loved our son. She stepped in when life felt unbearable. She showed up not just as a mother-in-love, but as a second mother, a grandmother, a protector, and a source of grace.

Her arms became a shelter for us when ours felt empty. Her words reminded me that I wasn't alone, even when my soul screamed otherwise. Her love for our son was fierce, unwavering, steady. She helped carry him through the trauma, giving him pieces of stability when his world had been shattered. That is the kind of love that is sacred. The kind that doesn't fade with tragedy, but instead grows stronger because of it.

She could have turned inward. She could have shut us out to nurse her own pain. But instead, she wrapped us inside of hers, holding us tighter, reminding us that even in the ashes, family remains.

For our son, she has been a light. For me, she has been a safe place. For both of us, she has been proof that love does not die when a life ends, it continues, reshapes, and becomes legacy.

To my mother-in-love: I love you. I honor you. I thank you for every single day you've chosen to keep loving me and our son, even through your own tears.

Your son may no longer walk this earth, but through you, and through our child, his love still lives on.

Letter to My Mother in Love

Dear Mother in Love,

There are no words big enough to describe how grateful I am for you. In one of the most painful moments of my life, when the world stopped and everything shattered, you were there. Not just as his mother, not just as my mother-in-law, but as a woman who knew grief and chose love anyway.

You stood beside me when I could barely stand. You comforted me when I didn't have the words to speak. You held space for both of us, me and the precious child your son left behind. You have helped me raise him when I didn't know how I'd do it alone. You've shown up for him in ways that only a grandmother could. In doing that, you've also helped me heal pieces of my heart I didn't know were still broken.

There's something sacred about the bond we share, born not of blood or title, but of pain, of strength, of love that refuses to give up.

I want you to know how much I love you.
How much I appreciate you.
How much I cherish you.

You lost a son, but you never lost your capacity to love, and because of that, your grandson still knows what family feels like, what safety looks like, and what legacy means.

Thank you for being the kind of woman he would be proud of. Thank you for being the kind of mother I admire. Thank you for being the kind of grandmother my son will never forget.

With all my heart,
Sherri

CHAPTER 12
"LOVE IN THE SHADOWS"

Healing isn't a straight line. Just when I thought I was moving forward, I met someone new. I was in the thick of healing when he came into my life. He came into my life when I was trying to stand again, when the ground under me was still shaky. I wasn't fully healed, but I was desperate for something soft, something safe. He said the right things. He showed up just enough to make me believe he cared. I clung to the idea of him. But the love wasn't real.

He wasn't honest
He wasn't consistent
And he wasn't who he pretended to be.

At first, he felt like my peace. He told me he loved me and I told him I loved him too, but the truth is, that wasn't love. Love doesn't lie. Love doesn't disappear without explanation. Love doesn't play with your emotions and call it care. He said the words, but he didn't live them. He looked me in the eyes, but he wasn't honest with his heart. I wanted so badly to believe him, so I said them back, even though deep down I felt the hollowness in those words.

I reached out so many times, trying to make sense of what we had, trying to hold onto something real. But there was no truth to hold onto. There was no safety in his love, only shadows. That's when I learned: words are not love. Presence is. Honesty is. Consistency is.

And what he gave me... wasn't love at all.

Eventually, I realized he was only pretending to hold space for my brokenness, when in reality, he was using it. He was emotionally unavailable. I saw it. I felt it. But a part of me still wanted to believe that maybe, just maybe, he'd stay. I was vulnerable and he took advantage of that. I opened up to him, told him things I had never told anyone. I shared the deepest parts of me, hoping he'd hold them gently. But instead, he held them just long enough to make me feel seen…then walked away when it no longer served him. He didn't have to hurt me loudly. He hurt me in silence, through distance, through inconsistency, through making me feel like I was too much.

I started shrinking myself again. Questioning my worth again, wondering if I was being too emotional, too needy, too broken. But here's what I learned. Just because someone offers you attention doesn't mean they're capable of love. Just because someone listens, doesn't mean they're safe. And just because I'm healing, doesn't mean I won't make mistakes. That relationship or whatever it was, was not a step backwards, it was a mirror. It showed me the parts of myself I still needed to protect. I deserved more. I deserve more. And now I know that love should never feel like begging. Love should never feel like punishment for being vulnerable. I didn't realize it at the time but I was vulnerable, and he saw it. I tried to convince myself otherwise. I gave him chance after chance to be better. To be different. To be a better version of himself.

I poured my heart out into messages, trying to reach him, trying to find the man I thought I loved. I wrote words that bled truth and begged for clarity. I waited for responses that never came, came too late, or came empty. Each message was a piece of me. Pieces that he ignored, overlooked, or treated like they didn't matter.

I replayed every moment in my head, searching for where it went wrong. When he finally disappeared, he didn't give me the dignity of an explanation. What made it harder was who he was to everyone else.

An educator.
A coach.
A mentor to many kids who looked up to him.
And yet, he didn't know how to love.
At least, not me.

How could someone pour into children every day, speak about growth, about guidance, about doing better and still play games with a woman's heart behind closed doors? I kept asking myself that, wondering if maybe I was the exception. The truth is, he wore a mask so well that even I believed his performance. He showed up for the world but he disappeared when it came to me. I gave him grace. I gave him chances. I reached out to fix what he broke and in return I got silence.
Just silence.

It wasn't just that he left but it was how he left. He was emotionally unavailable, emotionally manipulative and emotionally absent. He made me feel like I was asking for too much when all I wanted was clarity. The saddest part? I wasn't even asking to be loved. I was just asking to be treated with honesty, with decency, with care but he couldn't give me that. While his absence hurt, it also taught me something powerful: Anyone who makes you feel like you're too much is not enough for you. I learned not to chase closure. I learned not to beg for the bare minimum. I learned that sometimes silence is the answer. I didn't lose him. I released another layer of pain and that is also healing.

I regret not loving myself more. That has changed now. The next time love comes to my door it will have to meet the version of me that no longer abandons herself to be seen.

Reflective Journal Entry
"How Can You Teach Love and Still Withhold It"

He was supposed to be the safe one. A man of influence. Someone who spent his days building up kids, teaching discipline, confidence, and accountability.

And yet, he couldn't do the one thing I needed most from him: show up with honesty and loyalty.

I keep wondering how someone can pour into others while draining someone who loved them. How do you teach love and still withhold it?

I believed in the version of him the world saw. But behind closed doors, I got silence and confusion. I got lies dressed up as affection. I bent until I almost broke, because I thought maybe, just maybe, I wasn't trying hard enough. Now I see it, he was never trying at all. It hurts, it lingers, but it no longer defines me.

He wasn't love
He was a lesson.

Letter to Him
"To the Man Who Couldn't Show Up"

It's a strange kind of heartbreak to love a man who looks whole on the outside but is broken where it matters most. You could stand in front of classrooms, cheer from the sidelines, and guide kids through their struggles. You didn't know how to show up for me and every time you pulled away, it tore at me a little more. When it came to loving me, you couldn't.

NO LOYALTY IN HIS ACTIONS.
NO COMPASSION IN HIS CHOICES.
NO LOVE, JUST ABSENCE DISGUISED AS PRESENCE.

You let me believe we were building something real, when all you were doing was hiding behind the performance of who you pretended to be.

I reached out to you so many times, not just to fix things, but to understand, and every time you responded with silence. You left me hanging in the middle of my own healing, without closure, and without truth.

You didn't just hurt me, you manipulated me. You knew I was in pain. You knew I was vulnerable and instead of being a safe place, you became another wound I had to recover from.

You may never read this and that is okay. This isn't for you.
This is for me.

For the woman who finally knows she deserves more. For the woman who no longer chases what hurts. For the woman who now understands that real love doesn't leave you guessing.

I forgive myself for staying too long. I release you for the part you played in my journey. Your absence showed me my strength and that is a gift you didn't mean to give, but you did.

Journal Entry
"From that Season of Vulnerability"

I gave you the best parts of me, my trust, my heart, my vulnerability. I gave you the kind of love that doesn't come with conditions, and I showed up for you in ways I had never shown up for anyone else.

And still, it wasn't enough.

You took my openness and treated it like it was a weakness. You took my honesty and met it with half-truths. You took my loyalty and gave me uncertainty in return.

I poured into you, believing that love could heal what was broken in you, but instead I found myself breaking in the process.

I thought my love would be safe in your hands. But instead, it was handled carelessly, like something that could be set down when the weight felt too heavy.

I wanted you to see me, not just the surface, not just what I gave you, but me.

And though you told me you loved me, your actions told a different story.

You gave me heartbreak, but even in that heartbreak, I found my strength.

I keep asking myself why did I let him in?

Why did I believe him?
Why did I ignore my gut when it was screaming at me to walk away?

Maybe I just wanted to feel loved again.
Maybe I just needed someone to tell me I wasn't too broken.

What he gave me was not love, it was convenience. I'm mad at myself, but I'm also learning.

I needed this to remember what I will never accept again."

Letter To My Younger Self
"To the Me That Stayed Strong"

Sweet girl,

You carried weights no child should have had to hold. You held pain in silence, wore strength like armor, and convinced yourself that breaking was not an option.

I know how tired you were. I know how much you wanted someone to step in and save you. But when no one did, you saved yourself.

You were strong when life demanded it. You were strong when love disappointed you. You were strong when others walked away. And even when you thought you couldn't take one more step, you found a way forward. But here's what I want you to know now: you don't always have to be strong.

You deserve rest.

You deserve softness.

You deserve to fall apart and still be loved.

Your strength got me here. And because of you, I know how to survive. But because of healing, I now know how to thrive.

Thank you for never giving up, even when the world felt too heavy. Thank you for staying strong, even when no one noticed.

I love you.

I honor you.

And I will carry you with pride for the rest of my life.

With gratitude,

Me

Section 3: The Healing

Chapter 13
"Unlearning Survival"

I was so used to surviving that I forgot how to live. For years, survival was my only goal. Just get through the day. Just smile. Just push forward. Just hold it together.

Healing showed me something I wasn't ready for: that kind of survival can become a prison. I had built my identity around being strong, around not needing anyone, around staying quiet, around being "fine" no matter what. But I wasn't fine, I was exhausted, and disconnected. I was stuck in a loop always bracing for the next blow.

At some point, I had to ask myself: What if I could live without waiting for the worst to happen? What if I deserve more than just getting by?"

I started unlearning survival. I stopped over-explaining. I stopped apologizing for needing rest. I stopped carrying people who wouldn't even meet me halfway. I started setting boundaries. I started asking for help. I started speaking up even when my voice shook.

And guess what?

The world didn't fall apart when I chose me. I stopped measuring my worth by how much pain I could hold. I realized that peace is not something I had to earn, it was something I was allowed to choose.

I don't want to be strong like a soldier anymore. I want to be strong like a woman who feels deeply and still chooses to rise. I am unlearning survival. And in its place, I'm learning softness. I'm learning presence. I'm learning joy.

CHAPTER 14
"THE RETURN TO MYSELF"

After everything I'd been through, the grief, the trauma, the heartbreak, I realized something: I had spent so long trying to be loved, I forgot to love myself. I gave so much of my energy trying to fix others, prove my worth, earn loyalty, that I abandoned myself in the process.

Healing didn't happen all at once, but piece by piece, I started coming back to me. I started saying no. I stopped chasing people who made me question my value. I reconnected with my body, my mind, and my boundaries. I started walking differently, more grounded. I looked in the mirror and saw not what was missing, but what had survived. I no longer needed someone to complete me. I wasn't waiting for a savior. I became what I needed. The love I had been searching for was never out there, it was always waiting inside of me.

Now when I look in the mirror, I see more than scars, I see a survivor. I see a woman who can love without losing herself, a mother who chose life when death felt easier, a daughter who found forgiveness where there was once grief.

The return to myself is not a final destination. It is a daily choice to stand in my truth, to honor my healing, and to love myself in ways I once begged others to love me. It is a journey of becoming, and I am still walking it. This time I walk in peace.

This was the return. Not to the version of me before the pain, but to the version of me who rose through it.

And she is everything I prayed to become.

CHAPTER 15
"HEALING ISN'T PRETTY, BUT IT'S SACRED"

People think healing is soft, peaceful, gentle, but mine wasn't. Healing broke me down before it built me up. It was rage and crying on the floor and sitting in silence so loud it echoed. It made me cry at red lights. It made me cancel plans. It made me sit in rooms with people who didn't understand the weight I was carrying. It was learning how to be alone without being lonely. It was walking away from people I loved who didn't love me in the way I needed. It was sacred. And it was mine.

Healing isn't pretty. It isn't tidy. It isn't something that you post on social media with pretty quotes and flowers. Healing is raw. It's messy. It's nights when you cry so hard you can't breathe, and mornings when you wonder if it's even worth getting out of bed. Healing is facing the truth you spent years trying to bury. Healing is sacred because it requires surrender. You don't get to control how it unfolds, how long it takes, or what it demands of you. Healing has its own rhythm. Healing forced me to face myself, not just the hurt parts, but the bitter ones, the angry ones and the numb ones.

Some days it looks like crying until your body is empty. Other days it looks like laughing without guilt for the first time in years. Sometimes, it's just sitting in silence and realizing you survived. I had to look in the mirror and admit the truth: I'm not okay, but I want to be. I had days when I couldn't get out of bed. Nights where memories kept replaying and I had no off switch. I questioned God, I questioned love, I questioned myself. But I kept showing up.

I journaled even when my hands shook.
I cried in therapy.
I screamed into pillows.
I prayed through tears.

And somewhere in that sacred mess something shifted.

I stopped expecting healing to look like perfection. I started letting it look like whatever I needed that day, sleep, silence, writing, movement, tears, saying "no," choosing joy even when joy felt risky.

Healing didn't make me spotless.
It made me aware.
It made me honest.
It made me human.

There is nothing glamorous about grief. There is nothing cute about trauma. There is something holy about choosing to stay alive when everything inside you wants to give up. That is sacred. That is healing.

I don't pretend to be fully healed. I don't think anyone ever is, but I know this, every tear, every scream, every prayer has been sacred. I'm proud of every messy, beautiful step.

CHAPTER 16
"REWRITING THE STORY"

I used to think my story had already been written for me. The trauma, the abandonment, the grief, the emotional wounds passed down like an unwanted inheritance, but something changed. One day, I realized I could rewrite the story.

I didn't have to become bitter like my father. I didn't have to shrink myself to be loved. I didn't have to pass the pain to my son like a torch. I could choose the truth. I started parenting differently, I started speaking differently. I no longer saw my pain as a burden. I saw it as a blueprint.

Every time I hugged my son, I was undoing what had been done to me. Every time I said "I love you" without him earning it, I was rewriting my history. The story that was passed to me was one of silence, anger, and distance. The story I'm writing now is full of grace, honesty, boundaries and love.

This is how you break a cycle. Not with perfection, but with intention. I am no longer the scared little girl trying to earn her father's love. I am a grown woman, healing. A mother, loving freely. A survivor, speaking boldly.

And for the first time in my life, I'm holding the pen.

CHAPTER 17
"THE GIRL WHO CAME BACK TO LIFE"

There was a time I didn't recognize myself. I looked in the mirror and saw grief wearing my face. I saw trauma in my eyes. I saw a woman who had forgotten how to smile without flinching. I wasn't living, I was floating through pain. Somewhere between the silence and the breakdowns, the prayers and therapy, the heartbreak and the healing. I started coming back.

Not all at once.
Not in some magical moment.
But slowly.

I heard myself laugh again and didn't apologize for it. I danced in the kitchen without worrying who was watching. I forgave people who didn't say sorry, because I was tired of waiting. I began to speak. I told the truth about my pain. I let go of shame. I stood in rooms that used to trigger me and held my head high.

That little girl who used to hide, who used to cry herself to sleep, who used to wonder if she'd ever be enough. She came back. Wiser. Softer. Stronger. The world didn't give me peace. I found it in ruins. I learned that healing is not about becoming who you used to be, it's about remembering who you were always meant to be. The girl who almost gave up. She came back to life.

And this time, she's never leaving herself again.

CHAPTER 18
"BECOMING THE WOMAN, I NEEDED"

I didn't always know who I was. I was shaped by survival, by loss, by abandonment, by silence. I spent years searching for love in places that left me emptier than I began. I chased peace in people, comfort in chaos, and worth in the wrong hands. But underneath all of it, I was still there, buried, quietly waiting, and now, I've become the woman that broken little girl was praying for.

I am soft, but I am not weak.
I am queen, but I am not naïve.
I speak the truth even when it shakes the room.
I walk away from what doesn't honor me.
I nurture myself with the same care I once begged from others.

I've learned to mother myself. To protect my peace. To choose healing over chaos, even when it's lonely. I became the woman who holds space for her grief and her joy. The woman who makes her own closure. The woman who builds a life, not out of what she lost, but out of what she deserves.

I am not who I was, and I will never again apologize for who I've become. I am the healed version of every woman who thought her story was over. I am the woman I needed, and I am finally, fully home.

Letter To My Maternal Grandmother

Dear Grandma May,

Thank you! Thank you for being the steady love that I needed when life felt unsteady. Thank you for taking me into your arms when my mother couldn't be there, and for showing me what care, consistency, and protection truly looked like.

You loved me through every season, not with perfection but with presence. You gave me warmth when I felt cold, guidance when I felt lost, and discipline that I didn't always appreciate then but now understand as love.

When I look back, I see how much of my strength came from you. You taught me to stand tall even when my world felt small. You gave me roots when abandonment could have broken me.

I honor you not just as my grandmother, but as the woman who filled the role of mother in my life. The one who stayed. The one who carried me through.

I will forever dedicate this book, and this journey, to you. For every meal you cooked, every prayer you whispered, every time you chose me when others didn't, you will always be my foundation.

With eternal love and gratitude,

Your Granddaughter

Letter To My Paternal Grandfather

Dear Granddaddy,

Even though you are no longer here, your presence still lives within me. I carry your strength, your wisdom, and the quiet love you showed in your own way.

You were a man of resilience, a provider, and someone whose hard work spoke louder than words ever could. I remember the steadiness you carried, and even in the moments when life was heavy, you pressed on.

I want you to know how much I love you, and how much I appreciate all you did for me. You taught me that love is not always loud, but it is felt. You showed me that responsibility matters, and that family, even in its imperfections, is worth standing for.

Though I wish we had more time together, I hold on to the memories, the lessons, and the love. You are part of the foundation of who I am, and I honor you with every step I take forward.

Thank you for being my grandfather. Thank you for the sacrifices you made and for the example of perseverance you left behind. I will carry you in my heart always.

With love and gratitude,

Your Granddaughter

In Loving Memory
"Love, Loss and Legacy"

🌿 To my maternal grandmother:

Thank you for showing me what it means to stay when others walk away. You taught me strength when life wanted me to break. You were the one who showed me what it meant to stay, to nurture, to carry someone through storms. I am who I am because of you. Your legacy of love will live on every page of this book, and in every step moving forward.

🥃 To my father:

You were complicated. You were loud, harsh, and broken in your own ways. There were words you spoke that cut me deep and love I longed for that never came. But even in that absence, you taught me what kind of parent I would never be. Your struggles shaped me, and though your love is not what I needed, I honor the man you were. I forgive you and I release the pain and hold on to the lessons.

🚚 To my paternal grandfather:

Though you were on the road often, your presence was still a part of my foundation. You worked hard, and you took care of everyone. I know that you carried the weight of providing but you stepped in when my father couldn't. Your quiet strength still carries me. Your quiet strength remains with me, and I carry your memory with honor.

♥ To the love of my life:

You left this world too soon, and in a way I can never forget. The trauma of that moment shattered me, but the love we shared will always remain. You left me with heartbreak and the greatest gift of all, our son. Through him, a piece of you still lives, still breathes, and still matters. Through him you live on. Your absence is felt every day, but so is your love.

This book is not just my story; it is all of theirs too. Through it all, I have learned healing is never pretty, but it is sacred.

Journal With Me: Pain on Paper

Affirmations for the Healing Journey

- I am healing even when it doesn't feel like it.
- I deserve love that doesn't hurt.
- My scars are proof that I survived.
- I no longer carry what broke me.
- I honor my story by telling it.
- I am allowed to rest. I am allowed to rise.
- I am worthy of joy, not just survival.
- I forgive to free myself, not excuse the pain.
- I am the love I never received.
- I am no longer who I had to be to survive.
- My voice matters. My truth matters. I matter.

Reflection Prompts:

-Which affirmation speaks to your current season the most? Why?

_____
_____
_____
_____
_____

-What are you letting go of that no longer serves your healing?

_____
_____
_____
_____

-Describe a moment where you chose to love over pain.
_____
_____
_____
_____
_____

-Write a letter to your younger self and remind them what they survived.
_____
_____
_____
_____
_____

-What does healing look like for you today?
_____
_____
_____
_____
_____

-What truth are you finally ready to say out loud?
_____
_____
_____
_____
_____

-How has silence shaped your story, and what would you say if you could finally give it a voice?
_____
_____
_____
_____
_____

-Who are what have you grieved that still lingers in your heart?

_____
_____
_____
_____
_____

-Write about a time you felt abandoned or unseen. What did that experience teach you about yourself?

_____
_____
_____
_____
_____

-What do you need to forgive yourself for in order to move forward?

_____
_____
_____
_____
_____

-What scars do you carry that remind you not of pain, but of your strength?

_____
_____
_____
_____
_____

-What love did you wish you had received, and how can you give that love to yourself today?

_____
_____
_____
_____
_____

Reflection Note Pages

"Healing Between the Lines"
A space to release, reflect, and rewrite your story.

"From Pain to Purpose"
Notes that capture your growth through every emotion.

"Unfolding My Truth"
Write freely. Feel deeply. Heal fully.

"Reflections Beyond the Tears"
Your private place for honest healing and self-discovery.

"Soul Notes"
For the words your heart has been waiting to speak.

"Pages of Healing"
Because pain only loses its power when you write it down.

www.ingramcontent.com/pod-product-compliance
Lightning Source LLC
Chambersburg PA
CBHW060839190426
43197CB00040B/2712